STEP BY STEP PIANO LESSONS The Fun Way

MASTER SERIES 2

DR. GERALDINE LAW-LEE

© RHYTHM MP SDN. BHD.1994
New Edition 2003

Published by
RHYTHM MP SDN. BHD.
1947, Lorong IKS Bukit Minyak 2,
Taman IKS Bukit Minyak, 14100 Simpang Ampat,
Penang, Malaysia.
Tel: +60 4 5050246 (Direct Line), +60 4 5073690 (Hunting Line)
Fax: +60 4 5050691
E-mail: rhythmmp@mphsb.com
Website: www.rhythmmp.com

Cover Design by
Shamsul Anuar

ISBN 967-985-406-X
Order No.: MPS-4003-02

Photocopying Prohibited.
All rights reserved. Unauthorised reproduction
of any part of this publication by any means
including photocopying is an infringement of copyright.

☆CONTENTS☆

3	☆PREFACE☆
4	Imitation
	Allegro Moderato
5	Country Dance
6	☆SOME EARLY KEYBOARDS☆
	A Clavichord
	A Harpsichord
7	Prelude
8	Little Song
9	Etude in C
10	My Left Hand Etude
11	A Happy Morning (C major)
12	A Sad Afternoon
	Lento e Legato
13	☆THE EARLY 18TH CENTURY PIANO☆
14	Arioso
	Adagio
15	A Song
16	Russian Folk Song
	Con Spirito
17	Arietta In C Major
18	Tempo Di Minuetto
20	Gavotte In C
	Con Moto
21	Minuetto
22	Short Recital Classic
23	Happy Moments
	Cantabile
24	Another Recital Melody
25	The Old Windmilll
	poco cresc.
26	☆SOUNDS IN THE ROMANTIC PERIOD☆
27	Warm Ups In D
28	My Study In D
29	My Same Study With Some Variations!
30	Allegretto In D
32	Skating In D
33	Lullaby
34	☆THE CONTEMPORARY PERIOD (1900-PRESENT)☆
	Contemporary Styles In Music
35	My Mezzo Staccato Tune
36	Follow Me And Improvise
	Rhythm practice for
37	Fun Rows
38	☆MODERN KEYBOARDS IN THE 20TH CENTRY☆
	A Synthesizer
	A Portable Organ
	The Boogie Rat
	Medium Boogie
40	Alone
	sempre
41	My Little Jazz Piece
42	Skip In 2nds
43	The Little Chinese Maid
44	Quiet Island Of Malaysia
	Tranquillo
	gently
45	Misty
46	Fun Times
	Allegro e Scherzando
47	Peaceful Thoughts In The Evening
	dim. e rit.
48	A Dayak's Joy
49	The Can-Can
50	Danube Waves
	sempre staccato
52	Now Is The Hour
54	Di Tanjung Katong
56	March Of The Toreadors
	Alla Marcia
57	Hungarian Dance No. 5
58	Geylang Si Paku Geylang
60	Ikan Kekek
62	Toymaker's Dance
64	The Boogie

☆PREFACE☆

This is the 2nd stage of the Master Series for Pianoforte lessons, the fun and creative way. It is hoped, that, with gradual introduction to Classics in a more comprehensive way, students will enjoy learning classical pieces with the understanding of the background of the composers, the general trend of the period, the understanding of the different styles, the titles and meaning of the compositions and forms, as well as signs or terms that should be all integrated in the teaching of a new piece. Teachers are guided with questions and pupils have a guide to refer to. With better understanding of their pieces, students will surely play more musically and meaningfully. Suggestions are given for articulation but teachers may opt to change it if they wish. Pictures should be explained and related to what they are teaching. Right from the start if this approach is pursued fervently, pupils and teachers will see a different product in the performance of the pieces and their attitude towards Classical music as an enjoyable and educational culture to be treasured and appreciated.

Dr. Geraldine Law-Lee

Imitation

Allegro Moderato - means moderately lively.

DISCUSSION:

Discuss the tune in G and D major. Find them!

Make this sound as jolly as you can! Think of happy lads and lasses dancing on the village green. These staccato notes must be played with a crisp finger touch; keep the fingers firm at the tips and go well into the keys. Be careful with the slurred notes, make sure there is no break between them. The end of the slurred quavers must be light.

Country Dance

Allegro ♩ = 126

Müller

☆SOME EARLY KEYBOARDS☆

Below is a picture of a German clavichord. A clavichord is a soft keyboard developed in the 14th century. It has a very gentle tinkling sound which is produced by stopping the strings at different points. Imagine very soft tinkling sounds when you play early Baroque pieces.

A Clavichord

A Harpsichord

This harpsichord was made in 1650.
It has 2 manuals and its tone is bright,
short and cannot sustain.
Its strings are plucked by quills.
Many 17th century Baroque composers like
Purcell, Bach and Handel
wrote for the harpsichord.
Play the next piece thinking about
harpsichord sound (Short, detached,
plucked, bright sounds).

Think of the harpsichord sounds as you play this piece.

Prelude

Flowing

Henny Purcell

*N.B. ---- Note the line of interest in RH and then LH. Melody in both hands were common in The Baroque period.

Little Song

Dolce MM ♩ = 88

Christian Gottlob Neefe
(1748-1798)

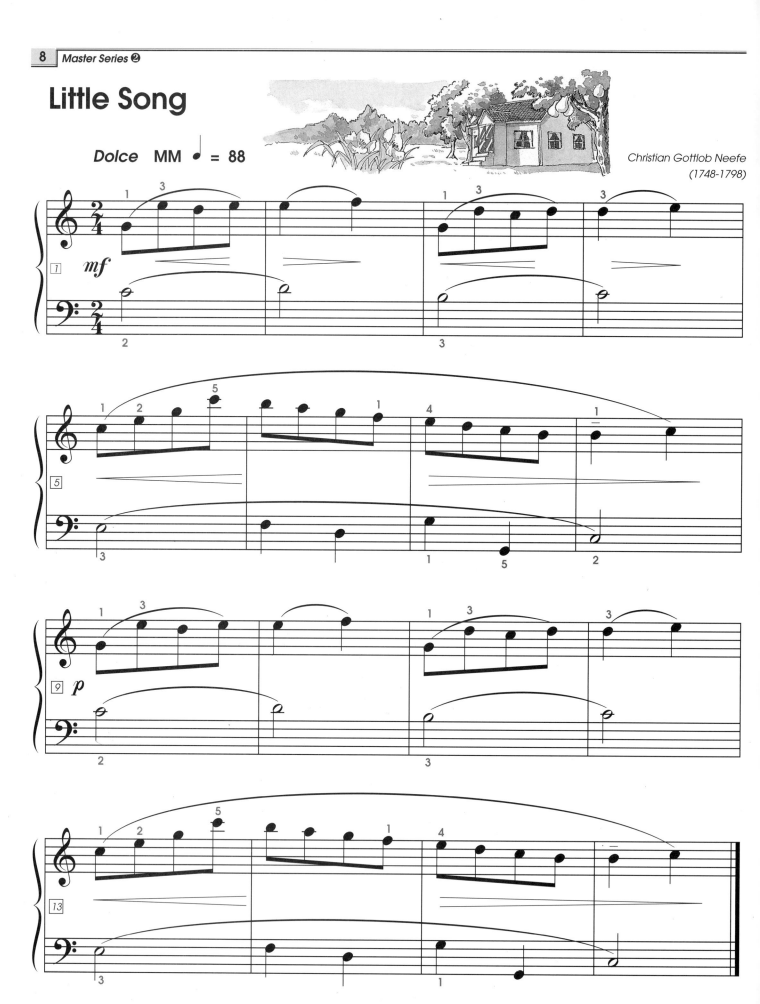

 **DISCUSSION:**

The phrases, how 1st and 3rd phrase differs? Chord formed by RH bar 5 and 13.

- An **Etude** is a study or exercise to train the technique of the player memorize page 9 and 10 and play it fast.

☞ *Presto* - means very fast.

Etude in C

Presto
G. Law-Lee

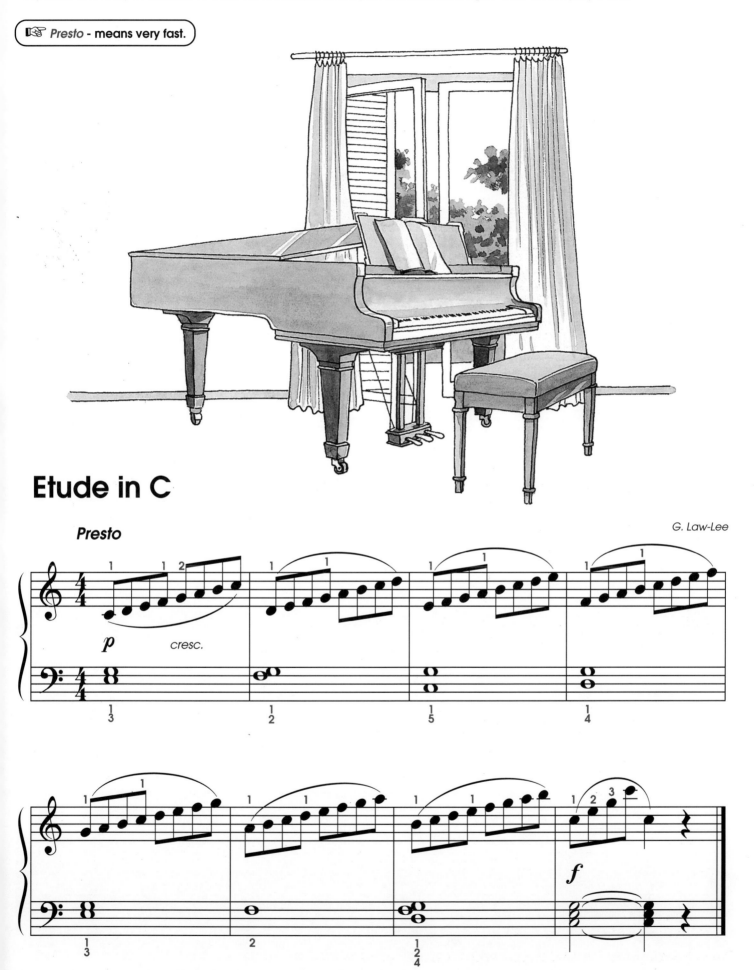

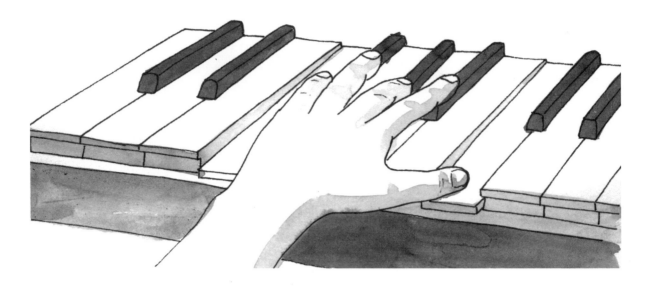

My Left Hand Etude

Presto

G. Law-Lee

CHARACTER PIECES.

A major key is often used to describe happy music. This is an imaginative piece. You must imagine or bring pictures to describe a happy morning.

A Happy Morning (C Major)

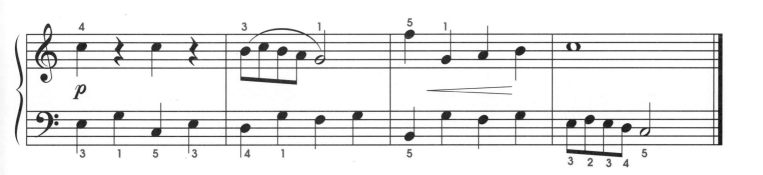

 **EXERCISES:**

1. How many times is this rhythm repeated? _____

2. What is the relative minor of C major? (A minor, D minor)

3. Picture a happy morning. Describe some of the things you can see or feel on a happy morning.

   a) The sun is (hidden, hardly seen, shining).

   b) The flowers are (blooming, dying, withering).

   c) You feel (sad, down, angry, bright and cheery).

   d) Your family feels (cheerful, sad, angry).

   e) The colours around you are (dull, light, bright).

   f) The air around you is (cold and damp, warm and fresh).

CHARACTER PIECES.

A minor key is usually used to write a sad tune. Bring some pictures to show your teacher a sad scene.
Discuss major/ minor chord difference and recognition.

A Sad Afternoon

Lento e Legato ♩ = 60

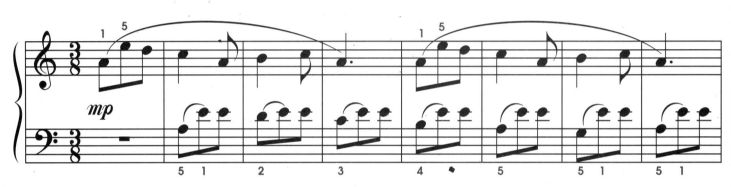

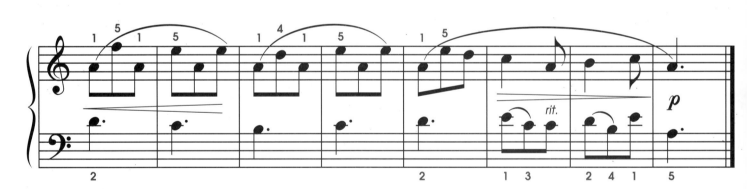

EXERCISES:

1. What does *cresc.* mean? _____
2. At what dynamic level does the piece end? Loud/ Soft
3. What key is this piece in ? A minor/ C major
4. Answer the following questions to describe a sad afternoon.
   a) The weather is (bright and sunny, cold and windy).
   b) When you look outside it is (dark and gloomy, bright and sunny).
   c) The colours around you are (bright, dull).
   d) People around you are (sad, happy, cheerful).
   e) Something (happy, boring, unfortunate) has just happened.
   f) The scene is (loud and festive, quiet and serious).

☆THE EARLY 18TH CENTURY PIANO☆

- small
- wooden frame
- 1 string to 1 key
- no pedals yet!
- not as many keys as our piano today.

The grand piano in the 18th century was small compared with the piano today and there were no pedals yet! This was what Mozart's piano looked like.

Arioso

- An **Arioso** is a little song. Sing the melody in the RH as you play. Keep a good flow.

☞ *Adagio* - means slow.

Adagio MM ♩ = 76

Daniel Gottlob Türk
(1756-1813)

Master Series ❷

CHARACTER PIECES.

Work at a good contrast of '*f*' and '*p*' and play it quite quickly.

☞ *Con Spirito* - means "With Spirit".

Russian Folk Song

Con Spirito

Ludwig Beethoven
(1770-1827)

- An arietta is a short song. Clementi was a very well known Italian classical composer who wrote many delightful keyboard works like sonatinas and sonatas.
Here you must imagine the right hand is a singer singing a short aria and left hand is the piano accompaniment.

Arietta In C Major

Allegretto ♩ = 100

Muzio Clementi
(1752-1832)

Imagine playing this piece on the harpsichord using upper keyboard for '*f*' and lower keyboard for '*p*' passages.

☞ *Con Moto* - means with movement.

Gavotte In C

Con Moto ♩ = 120

James Hook, Op.81
(1746-1827)

 **EXERCISES:**

1. How many sections are there in this piece? ____
2. In which bars can you find imitation? _____

- A **Minuetto** is a short minuet dance in triple time.

Minuetto

♩ = 108

C. H. Wilton
(1571-1621)

Short Recital Classic

Moderato ♩ = 104

Le Couppey
(1811-1887)

Try to play with a sweet singing tone, even in the soft passages. The phrasing is very important; think of the slur endings as breathing places. Control the tone carefully at the crescendos and diminuendos, just as the voice would rise and fall in singing. The left hand has a little tune, too, which must be gently sustained.

☞ **Cantabile** - means in a singing style.

Happy Moments

Cantabile ♩ = 112 - 116

Diabelli

Master Series 2

We know this piece is written in the Classical style because there is a simple melody and accompaniment.
Le Couppey was a French composer.
The broken chords in LH should be played softly and evenly.

Another Recital Melody

Le Couppey
(1811-1887)

☆SOUNDS IN THE ROMANTIC PERIOD☆

The grand piano in the 19th century was able to control louder and softer sounds.
The pedals were improved and used more by 19th century composers.
Compare this piano to the Baroque harpsichord and Mozart's piano.
Look at the pedals! It was bigger and had more keys!

An orchestra in the 19th century was much bigger.
Sounds were louder. Instruments were improved.

Warm Ups In D

G. Law-Lee

Play the D major scale and D major chord.

My Study In D

Moderato ♩ = 120 -126

Kohler

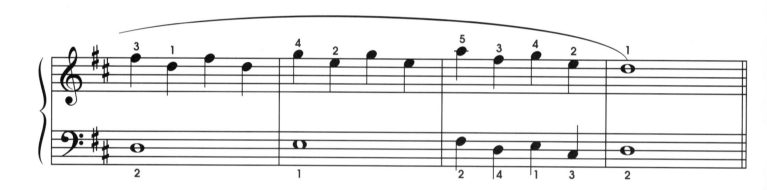
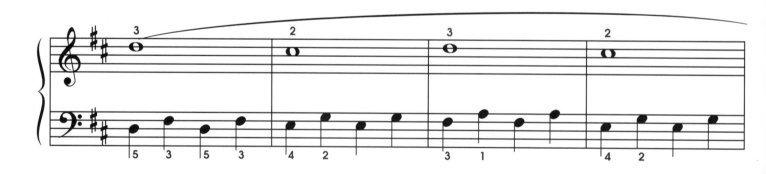
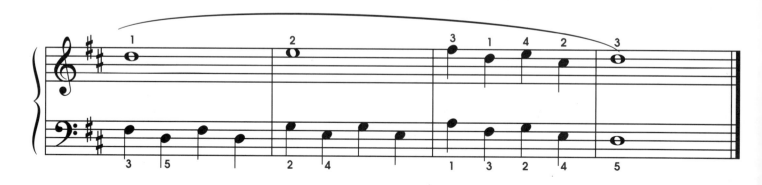

My Same Study With Some Variations!

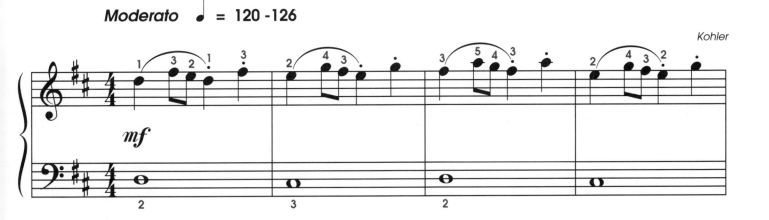

Allegretto In D

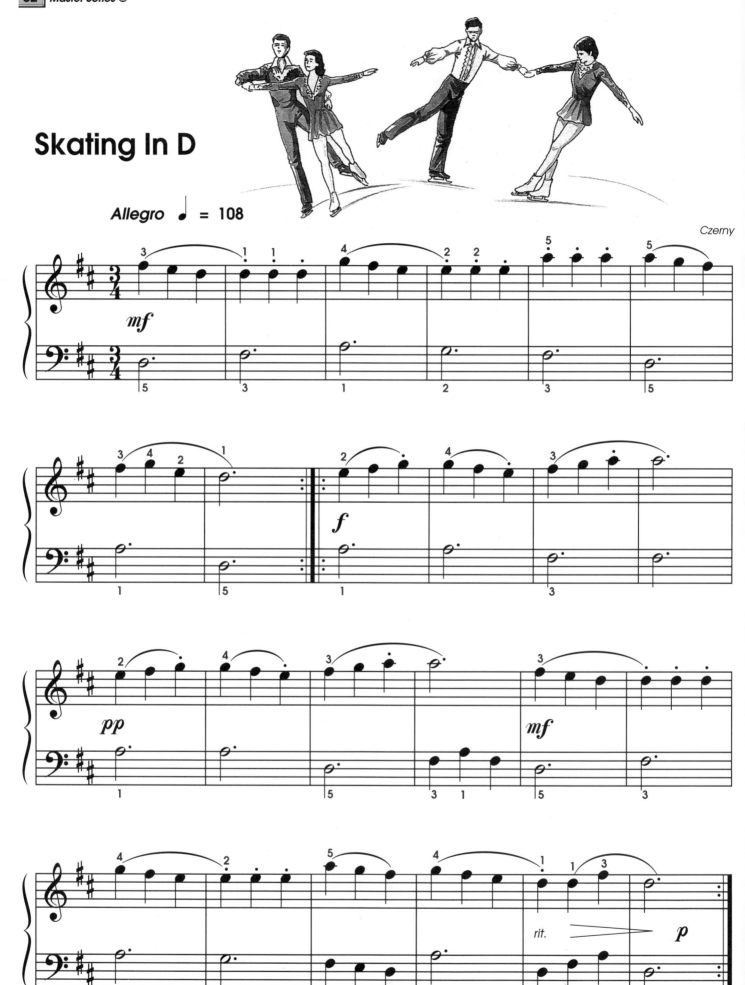

☆THE CONTEMPORARY PERIOD (1900 - PRESENT)☆

From 1900 onwards, there was a burst of modern, mechanized age.
Buildings became very angular and avant garde with odd shapes such as triangles and squares. Black and white or sudden bright colours became the favourites. Modern dresses were simple and practical. A lot of it became sleek and elegant or wild and odd. Styles varied tremendously. There was an outburst of electronic instruments and sounds.

Contemporary Styles in Music

There was a play on rhythm, percussive sounds and accents, variable bar lines (irregular measures), dissonance and abrupt shifts. There was also a lot of imaginative titles and modern day glassy sounds.

Modern day composers included:

Bartok	Kabalevsky	Shostakovich
Prokofiev	Stravinsky	Ravel
Debussy	Gershwin	Copland

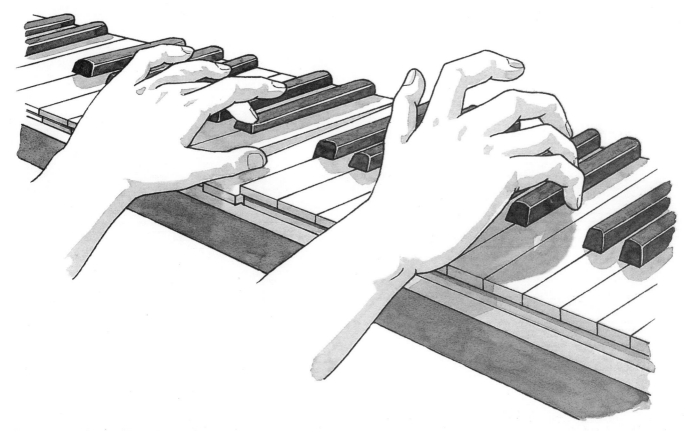

Bass Walk Swing

Compare bars 1 and 2 to bars 3 and 4. Listen carefully and you will find that bars 3 and 4 is actually the same as bars 1 and 2 but written with a little variation.

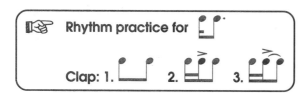

Follow Me And Improvise

G. Law-Lee

The Contemporary piano is larger and more resonant than the piano in the Romantic Period. The modern grand piano has a brilliant and powerful tone necessary for performance in today's large concert halls. It is very sensitive and can be controlled from pp to fff.

Fun Rows

☆MODERN KEYBOARDS IN THE 20TH CENTRY☆

If you have any of these, you may try this next piece with a boogie or swing rhythm to give this piece a swinging feel!

A Synthesizer

A Portable Organ

The Boogie Rat

Medium Boogie

G. Law-Lee

*N.B. ---- Play the **gliss** with the 4 fingers of the right hand, nails to the keyboard.

CHARACTER PIECES.

This piece needs imagination. The mood must be reflective, quiet and still.
A piece you like to play when you want something peaceful.

☞ *Sempre* - **means always.**

Alone

G. Law-Lee

A Digital Piano can be played perfectly like an acoustic piano or be played with a variety or orchestral sounds. It can even be played with a rhythm for jazzy pieces!

My Little Jazz Piece

G. Law-Lee

A second is a dissonant sound. Composers used a lot more 2nds and 7ths in the 20th century than before.

Skip In 2nds

Play the right hand gently and listen carefully to the intervals.

The Little Chinese Maid

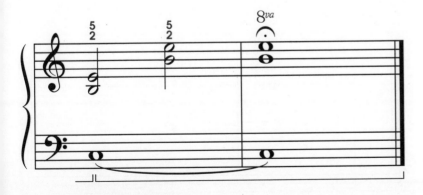

1. What interval is dominant throughout the RH ? _____

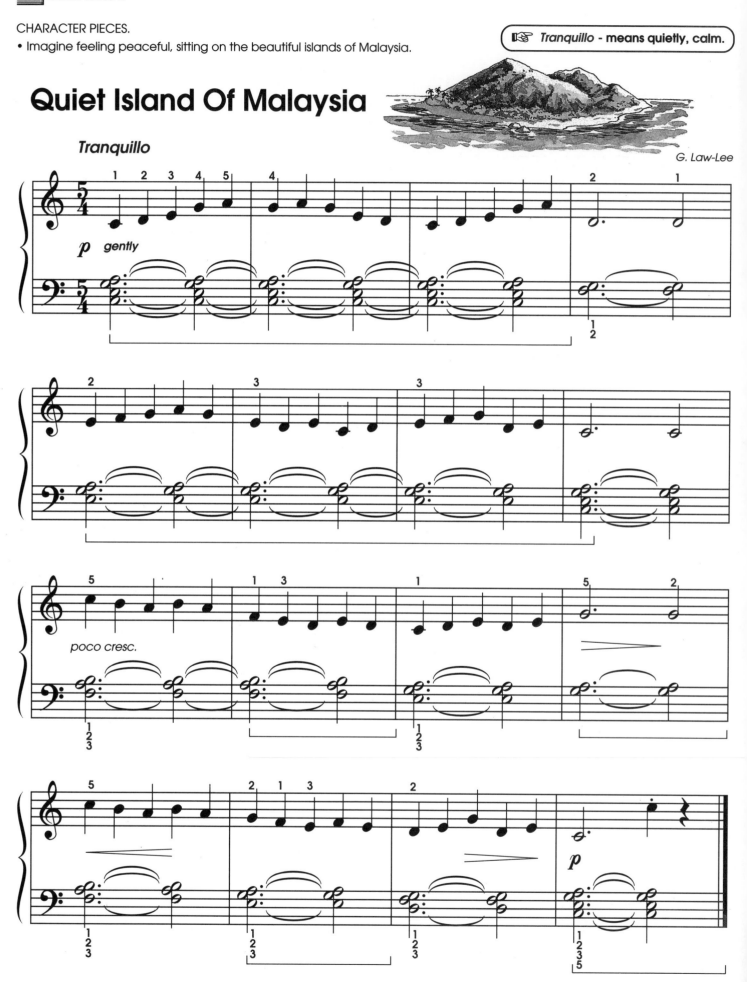

CHARACTER PIECES.
- Imagine a cool misty morning with foggy skies.

Misty

Leggiero e Lento

G. Law-Lee

pp

Keep pedal down throughout

rit.

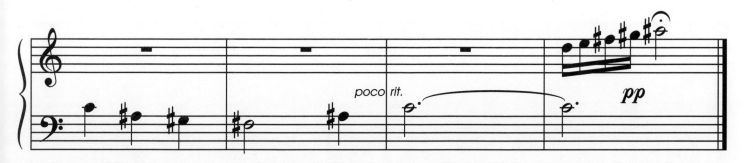

poco rit.   *pp*

*N.B. ---- Play this piece extremely softly throughout to create faraway misty impressions.

☞ *Allegro e Scherzando* - means lively and playful.

Fun Times

Allegro e Scherzando

G. Law-Lee

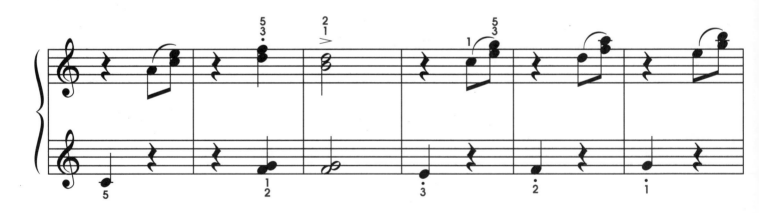
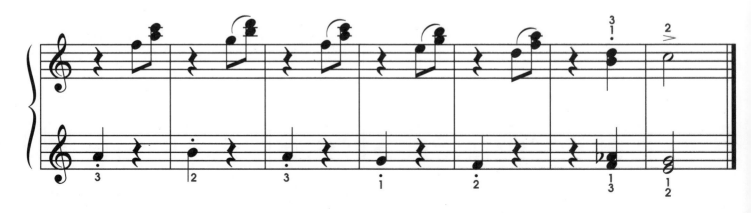

CHARACTER PIECES.

☞ *dim e rit.* - means getting softer and slower.

Peaceful Thoughts In The Evening

G. Law-Lee

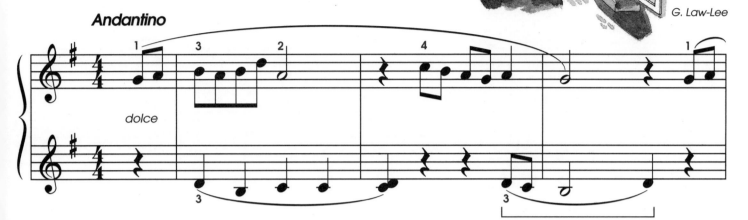
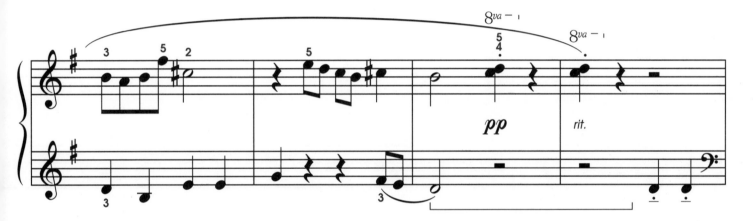
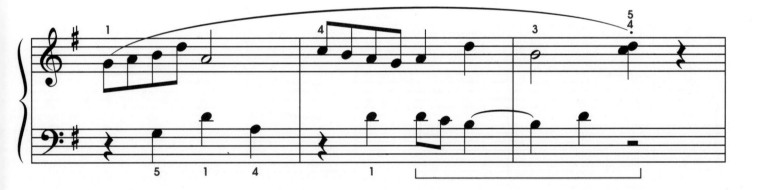

What do you notice in the left hand?

A Dayak's Joy

G. Law-Lee

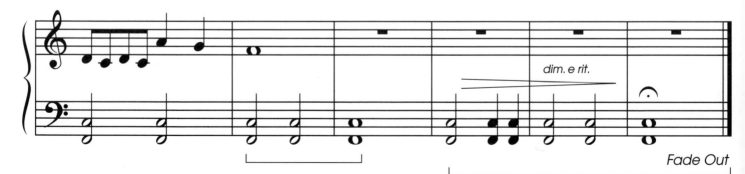

dim. e rit.

Fade Out

The Can-Can

Allegro

 **EXERCISES:**

1. What key is this piece in? _____

2. Name the key signature of this piece.

   _____

3. Can you see there are only 2 changes of chords in the left hand of this piece? They are _____ chord and _____ chord. (D F# A and A C# E G)

☞ *sempre staccato* means always staccato.

Play LH lightly!

Danube Waves

Moderato

J. Ivanovici

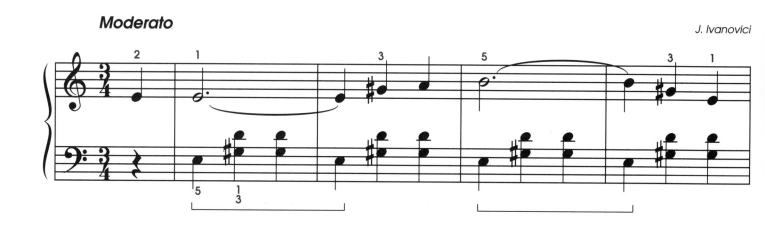

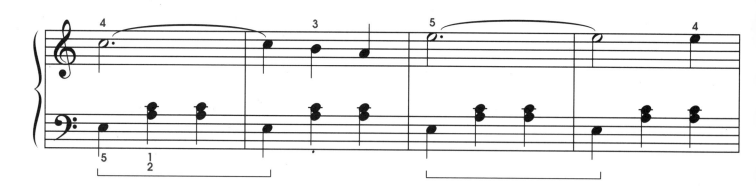

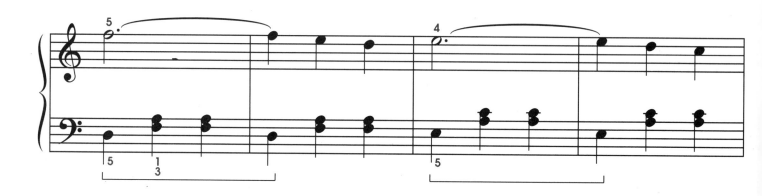

Now Is The Hour

*by Maewa Kaihan,
Clement Scott and
Dorothy Seward*

Adagio

Now is the hour when

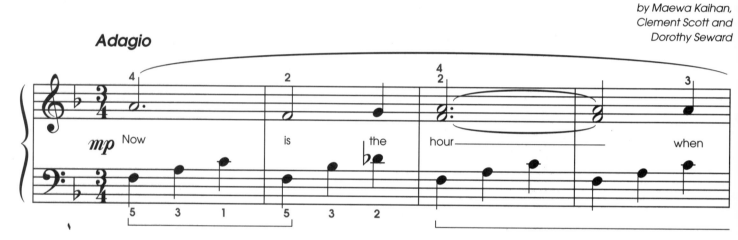

we must say good-bye;

Soon you'll be sail - ing

Di Tanjung Katong

Allegretto ♩ = 100

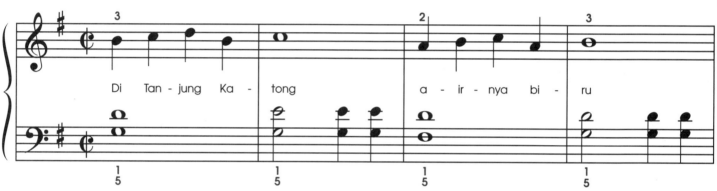

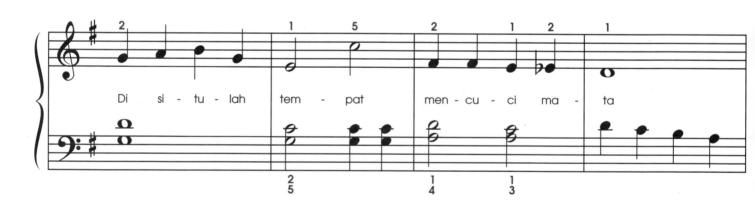

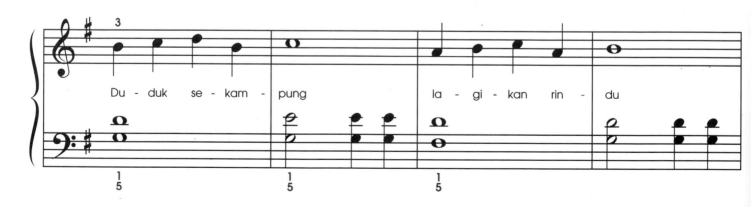

Master Series ❷

Talk about the air of grandness, majestic and proud moments!

☞ *Alla Marcia* - means in the style of a March.

March Of The Toreadors
(from the opera "Carmen")

Alla Marcia

Georges Bizet
(1838-1875)

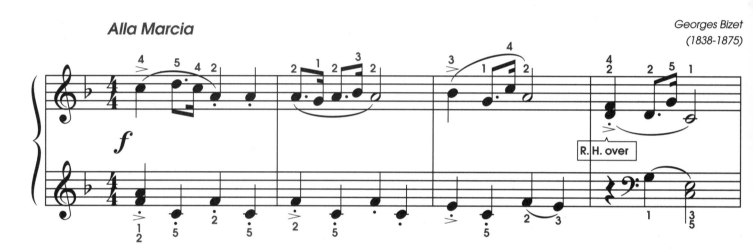

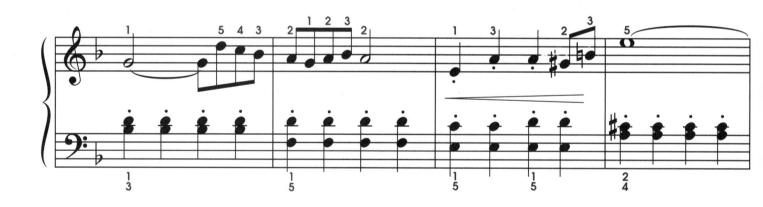

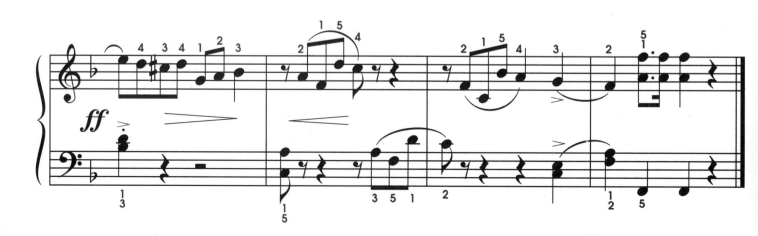

Geylang Si Paku Geylang

Asean Traditional

♩ = 108

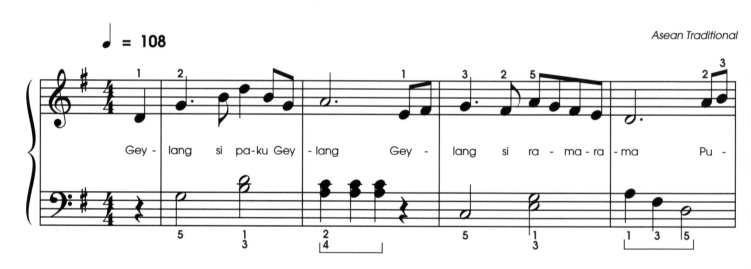

Gey- lang si pa-ku Gey- lang Gey- lang si ra - ma - ra - ma Pu-

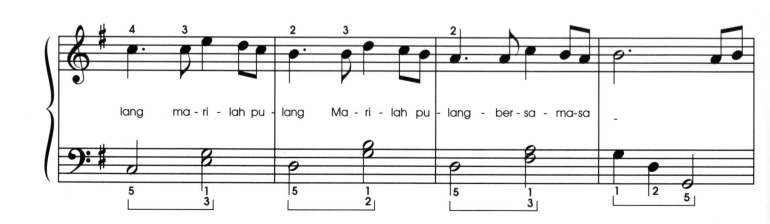

lang ma-ri-lah pu- lang Ma - ri - lah pu- lang - ber - sa - ma-sa -

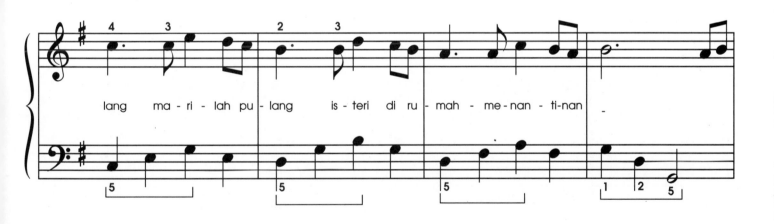
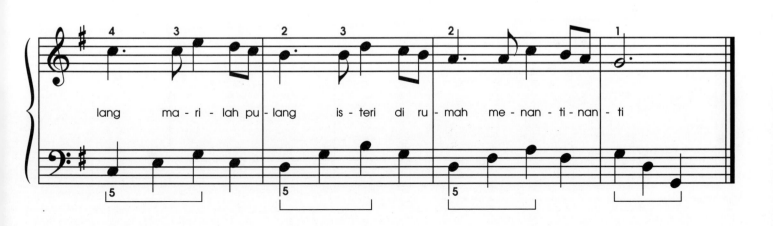

Ikan Kekek

♩ = 120

Malaysian Traditional

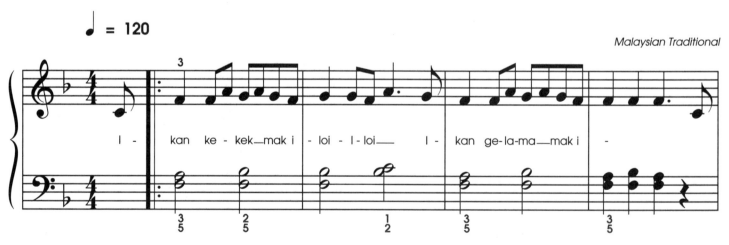

I - kan ke - kek — mak i - loi - i - loi   I - kan ge - la - ma — mak i -

ti a - dik — mak-i - loi i - loi   Pu - lang sa - ma — Mak i -

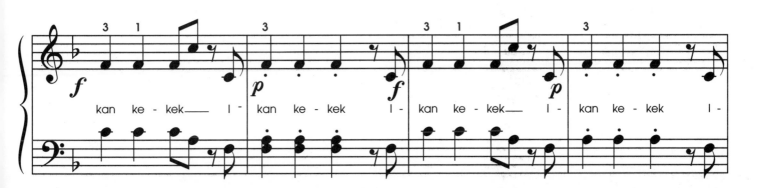
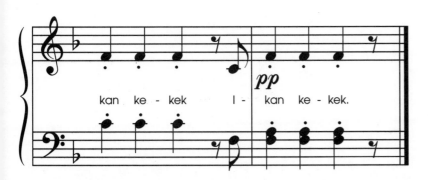

EXERCISES:

1. What key is this piece in? _____

2. Is there any change of key? _____

Toymaker's Dance

Moderato

English Round

Both hands

DISCUSSION:

Discuss the 3 sections in this piece and the melodies in 1st and 3rd bar of section B.